STARTUP FOR EVERYONE

STARTUP FOR EVERYONE

*Translating Tech Startup Concepts
for Everyone Else Starting Stuff*

Casey Bankord

Chicago, IL

© 2020 CAB VENTURES, LLC
Printed in the United States of America
Author: Casey Allen Bankord
Editor: Nicole King
Cover Design: Dustin Bankord and Jason Kleist
ISBN: 9798656983129

"It is not the critic who counts; not the man who points out how the strong man stumbles, or where the doer of deeds could have done them better. The credit belongs to the man who is actually in the arena, whose face is marred by dust and sweat and blood; who strives valiantly; who errs, who comes short again and again, because there is no effort without error and shortcoming; but who does actually strive to do the deeds; who knows great enthusiasms, the great devotions; who spends himself in a worthy cause; who at the best knows in the end the triumph of high achievement, and who at the worst, if he fails, at least fails while daring greatly, so that his place shall never be with those cold and timid souls who neither know victory nor defeat."

– Theodore Roosevelt

Contents

Introduction – Why *Startup for Everyone?* ix

Define 1

1. **10-Slide Deck** 3
   How do I write a business plan?
2. **TAM-SAM-SOM** 7
   How do I know how big my idea is, and how can it get bigger?
3. **Minimum Viable Product (MVP)** 13
   How do I test my idea before risking too much?
4. **Exit Strategy** 19
   How do I make sure I'm building something valuable?
5. **Incorporation** 23
   How do I set up the business entity correctly?

Design 29

6. **Hacker, Hustler, Hipster** 31
   How do I build the right founding team?
7. **Vesting & Cliffs** 35
   How do I divide ownership among co-founders?
8. **Convertible Debt** 41
   How do I raise money before I know what my business is worth?
9. **Alpha & Beta** 47
   How do I win customers when I'm new and unproven?
10. **Value Metric** 51
    How do I determine the right pricing?

Develop ... 55

11. Burn Rate ... 57
  How do I not run out of money?

12. Pivot ... 61
  How do I stay in business if my first idea is failing?

13. Adoption Curve ... 67
  How do I determine who my target customer should be?

14. Personas ... 73
  How do I avoid trying to be everything to everyone?

15. Technical Debt ... 79
  How do I stay organized and build something solid?

Drive ... 83

16. A/B Testing ... 85
  How do I know the right way to sell my product/service?

17. Conversion Funnel ... 89
  How do I find more customers predictably?

18. Onboarding ... 95
  How do I ensure customers have a great experience?

19. LTV vs. CAC ... 101
  How do I know how much I should spend on marketing?

20. Product Market Fit ... 105
  How do I know the right time to "go big"?

Bonus Chapter – Definitions on Additional Terms
  CAP Table, MRR, EBIT, Lean Startup, Prototyping, P&L, Balance Sheet, Growth Hacking, Bootstrapping, Term Sheet, Pro Forma ... 109

Conclusion – My hope for you ... 111

About the Author – Casey Bankord ... 113

Why *Startup for Everyone*?

Business ownership can be one of the most thrilling and rewarding experiences in a professional career. Generally, people intuit that fact, but for many aspiring starters there are often unseen barriers to taking the first step. Tech startups have become the latest "shiny object." For those without technical abilities, however, there is an even wider perceived chasm to that first step to achieving their dreams.

When I started my first business, my only professional experience up to that point was as a pastor. I felt like a fake in the business realm and I know I am not alone. I've met too many people recently who are intimidated by the specifics of starting "that thing"—that idea, that company, that non-profit. Whatever it is. They stumble across terms they don't understand. They are asked questions to which they don't have answers. They become overwhelmed with where to start. And their dream remains stifled.

Truth: There is a lot of wisdom available to guide these people.

Problem: Many of the best, most powerful startup concepts are written for tech companies.

Truth: Most new businesses in the U.S. are not tech startups.

Problem: Small(er) businesses like restaurants, local grocery stores, interior design firms, local non-profits, and even people within large companies who have an idea often find it difficult to get answers on how to start things—in words that make sense to them and in their context.

Startup for Everyone

I have started and built stuff, coached small business owners in starting and building stuff, and worked with large companies to start and build stuff. I have spent years in tech startups and also worked with people in non-tech business. I'd like to help close this wisdom gap and make all the most helpful concepts accessible to all.

I've written this short book, *Startup for Everyone*, with this goal in mind. This book is intentionally NOT written to tech startup founders. It is aimed at translating some of the great tactics those leaders deploy for everyone else starting stuff.

I have separated the book into four sections, each representing a critical phase of starting and building something successfully. First, define what you are doing, why you are doing it, and for whom you are doing it. Second, design a business that will accomplish your goals and also solve a problem for people. Third, develop your business in a way that mitigates risk and ensures a solid foundation for growth. Finally, drive your business to its full potential in a way that is sustainable. Define, design, develop, drive!

I'm excited about this, and I hope it is helpful to you.

DEFINE

What you are doing, why you are doing it,
and for whom you are doing it.

How do I write a business plan?
(10-Slide Pitch Deck)

1

How do I write a business plan?

What do you picture when you hear the words "business plan"? In my experience, most people envision a thick stack of paper in a large, three-ring binder with color-coded section dividers. They see complicated spreadsheets, long paragraphs of text, and impressive graphs that explain a perfectly thought-out strategy. And because of this mental picture, most business ideas go nowhere. They sit idle because they never get past the "who is going to write the business plan?" step.

Over the past 10 years, Silicon Valley tech startups have ditched the 100-page business plan. There were too many ideas, too many binders, and not enough time to read them all. Additionally, investors finally admitted that they typically skimmed through the 100 pages anyway to find several key bits of information that gave them confidence the idea or business had merit. Founders caught on to this, and thus the 10-slide pitch deck was born.

Tech Startup Term: "10-Slide Pitch Deck"

Startup for Everyone **Translation:** Ten pages that each answer a specific question in a succinct format.

Page 1: Elevator Pitch
This page should contain a memorable, punchy statement that introduces your idea quickly. This is something you could literally explain

in a 10-floor elevator ride. One silly example might be: "We are the Starbucks of Frozen Yogurt." (Not that anyone would choose that statement, but it's simple to understand.)

Page 2: The Problem
Every idea must solve a problem. This problem should be a real one that *has* to be solved. Otherwise, what's the point? This page should clearly state the problem and the importance of solving it.

Page 3: The Solution
Explain a solution (product or service) that specifically addresses the problem. Also, discuss why your proposed solution is better than the way people are solving this problem today. Why should they change?

Page 4: The Market
This page should prove that either many people have this problem occasionally OR a niche of people has this problem often. And even better, many people have this problem often.

Page 5: Business Model
You don't need a detailed financial plan here. You need a "back of the napkin" explanation of how you will charge for the product/service and what it costs you to make/deliver it. If this is a non-profit, you need to explain clearly how you will attract donations and for what reason.

Page 6: The Competition
Outline who else is trying to solve this problem, and why you think you are better suited to solve it. Or, explain how the competition is inadequately solving the problem. And, no, there is no such thing as "no competition." There is always competition—even if it is the status quo.

Page 7: Go to Market
Define how you plan to win customers. Oftentimes, the best way to do this is to describe your ideal customer (who most significantly

experiences this problem) and explain how you think you can attract that type of person to your product/service/experience. Then discuss how you plan to build momentum off your early customers.

Page 8: Financial Projections
If you combine page 4 (The Market) with page 5 (Business Model) and page 7 (Go to Market), you should be able to come to some rough estimates of how much money you expect to make/spend with your early customers and then on a larger scale. At this point, no one is looking for month-by-month projections. They (and you) want to know: 1) What can you do in the short term? 2) What can you do in the long term? Everything in the middle is a guess.

Page 9: The Team
This page is often titled "Why us?" because you need to define why you (and your team) are the *right* people to solve this problem with your solution. The right problem + the right solution + the right team = powerful combo. Research shows this is the second most viewed page by investors (after projections). What experience/skills/perspective do you bring that will make this idea work?

Page 10: The Ask/Need
Clearly articulate what is standing in the way of this concept going from just an idea to a real thing. Sometimes, it's money. Oftentimes, it's not. What resources/commitments/realities need to be in place to make this a go? What is your plan to resolve them?

Bottom Line
If you can build a one-page answer for each of these questions, you have a business plan. Sure, you can build it out into more detail, but most of the time that's not necessary. Even if you have no plans to raise money, going through this exercise is massively beneficial to you as you evaluate whether or not you have something good. Spend a weekend; crank it out. Move on to the next step of building your thing.

How do I know how big my idea is, and how can it get bigger?
(TAM-SAM-SOM)

2

How do I know how big my idea is, and how can it get bigger?

Ideas all start the same size—fragments of information stitched together as a concept in a person's mind. But once the idea is defined a bit more, the next natural question is: how big could this idea be? How many people or businesses might want this type of solution? And how big of a company could I build? Many ambitious entrepreneurs initially think, "This is going to be HUGE!" or some version of that sentiment. On the other end of the spectrum, more conservative entrepreneurs initially think, "Nah, there aren't enough people with that problem" and discard the idea. Either could be true, but how do you know?

Ironically, many of the "smallest" ideas have ended up being some of the biggest successes. For example, Whole Foods started as a niche natural foods store in Austin, and was eventually bought by Amazon for $14B; the toymaker Mattel started by making picture frames and now is valued at nearly $5B; and Burt's Bees was originally a candle maker that was bought by Clorox for nearly $1B. In contrast, some of the "biggest" ideas end up having little to no value (like many of the dotcoms of the late 90's).

How do I know how big my idea is, and how can it get bigger?

Tech entrepreneurs often require venture investments to pursue opportunities and/or scale their early-stage startups. As part of that process, potential investors have been helpful in establishing a rigorous, repeatable way to ask for an estimate of market size to justify their investment, the company's valuation, and the expected return on their investment. Businesses have been sizing their markets since the beginning of time; however, the tech startup markets have helped establish a clear, shorthand way to describe what is often misunderstood as a very complicated, elaborate task.

Tech Startup Term: "TAM-SAM-SOM"

Startup for Everyone **Translation:** Three numbers that will help you determine the overall size of your industry, pool of potential customers, and the percentage of those customers who will buy from you.

Sizing a market is something that could potentially make your eyes glaze over if you're not an MBA or a nerdy finance type (like me!). There has to be a better way, and—Good News! —there is. The TAM-SAM-SOM framework helps you quickly understand how big your idea might be, and even more importantly, it can give you the information you might need to *make your idea bigger*. To start, let's unpack what the acronyms stand for.

TAM (**T**otal **A**ddressable **M**arket) is the total number of customers who buy this kind of product or service. For a hair salon, this would be everyone who pays for a haircut in the country.

SAM (**S**erviceable **A**ddressable **M**arket) is the group of customers who *could* buy from you. For the hair salon, this would be everyone who pays for a haircut within a 15-mile radius of the salon.

SOM (**S**erviceable **O**btainable **M**arket) is the group of customers who actually will buy from you. This would be everyone who becomes a regular customer of the salon.

NOTE: The SOM is the number that will help you determine **how big YOUR business can be** vs. the size of the total industry.

Why do this? Does it even matter? YES. I used the hair salon example for a reason; it illustrates an important point about how you can GROW your idea when you challenge convention in each of these components. Once you know your TAM-SAM-SOM, you can play with the variables to drastically change the numbers.

For example, using the hair salon illustration above, you could challenge your TAM by saying, "How many people *don't* pay for haircuts but *would* pay for haircuts (or more haircuts) if X variable changed?" (Maybe it didn't take so much time, or people had help determining a hair style they wanted, etc.) An example of this kind of challenge could be the new company DryBar, who realized that people would visit a salon JUST to get their hair "blown out" instead of waiting for their next haircut for this beloved service.

You could also challenge your SAM by asking, "How many more customers could I reach if my salon was on wheels?" (Perhaps you could put it on a renovated RV or bus.) That would drastically change the geographical reach of your salon. Blood banks, dentist offices, and others have all been employing this tactic for years to expand their reach.

And then as your TAM and SAM grow, your SOM (total number of customers who will eventually buy from you) potentially grows with it. Most successful business ideas originate from founders who took established industry paradigms (oftentimes in what were previously considered small or unimportant industries), and became curious about what establishes a customer, and where the problems might be. You can do the same. But first, it is extremely helpful to go through the TAM-SAM-SOM process to start on the right path.

How do I know how big my idea is, and how can it get bigger?

Bottom Line
It might be tempting to classify "market sizing" as busy work in the grand scheme of things. You might not trust your ability to do it well. Don't buy into that myth. You can, and you should. Understanding the size of your business helps you design your business with accuracy from the beginning, while creating more opportunity than you ever thought possible when the idea first occurred to you.

How do I test my idea before risking too much?
(Minimum Viable Product)

3

How do I test my idea before risking too much?

Every new idea is "half-baked." That may be hard to hear, but it's true. Your idea, as good as it sounds to you, is 50–80% wrong. But, good news! You are not alone. Uber once believed that it would own a fleet of Mercedes-Benz vehicles with hired drivers to provide a car service for high-end customers. You can see the essence of what Uber is today within that concept, but they've obviously adjusted quite a bit along the way.

The fact that your idea isn't perfect is not a showstopper. It is also not a reflection of your competence (often a major source of insecurity for first time founders). Too often, people with new ideas start finding flaws in their idea, get discouraged, and then give up. Or they spend *way* too much time, effort, and money making their idea/concept/product perfect (in their own minds) and then launch, and no one cares. Innovation is most often a result of making half-baked ideas better, more valuable, and more relevant through a process of trial and error.

Tech startups have all begun taking a different approach, with a bias toward trial and error instead of building something perfect to launch. It wasn't always this way, but it most certainly is now. Today, a founder says that his or her idea is imperfect in a tone of pride. Eric

How do I test my idea before risking too much?

Reis, author of the book *Lean Startup*, coined a phrase to name this new approach, and it has become cemented within startup speak.

Tech Startup Term: "Minimum Viable Product (MVP)"

Startup for Everyone **Translation:** The most basic form of an idea that can be tested with customers.

I don't know who originally said, "Overnight successes are ten years in the making," but that statement certainly is true. Take Zappos, for example. In 1999, the founders believed (contrary to public opinion) that they could sell shoes online. The temptation would have been: 1) Listen to all the experts who said it would be impossible and give up; or 2) Become overly confident in the idea and spend significant money, time, and effort building a website, designing a brand, acquiring inventory, raising money, etc.

Instead, here are the steps they took:

1. *Minimum.* Nick, Tony, and Alfred created a simple website, "ShoeSite.com," in a weekend (you can do this too with a templated website builder like SquareSpace).
2. *Viable.* They went to the local shoe store, took pictures of all the shoes on the wall, and posted the pictures online with prices.
3. *Product.* They sold the shoes online, and then took that money back to the shoe store, bought the shoes at retail prices, and sent them to the customer.

They made absolutely no money with this approach, but they got something even more valuable in return. They learned that people *do* buy shoes online. They also learned what shoes were most popular, which sizes are bought most frequently, and what people's expectations were related to customer service. From that foundation, they could invest more into building their company.

The **minimum viable product** approach is simple. And you can do it.

Minimum. What is the core belief within your idea that if proven right will give you more confidence you've got something? For Zappos, it was that people would buy shoes online. What is yours? Once you define that, design a way to test that belief spending little to no money.

> *Example:* You want to start a bakery. Build a menu of items, bake them, invite a bunch of people over, give them monopoly money, and have them make selections. You'll learn what is most popular, get feedback on flavors and presentation, and have the opportunity to ask them about what they might want in a local bakery.

Viable. The test you design must be possible and practical within a short period of time. This is where people most often get stuck because they get overwhelmed by trying to pull together all the pieces that would make their product *perfect*. Instead of getting discouraged, ask yourself, "What *could* I do in a short period of time?"

> *Example:* You want to start a landscaping business. You are stuck because you don't have all the equipment you need to provide the service level you have in mind and it would cost thousands of dollars to acquire it. Go out and sign five customers for a one-time free landscaping service, *rent* the equipment you need to do a good job, deliver the service, and then ask for a weekly contract. Land the deals, then go buy the equipment.

Product. This is the trickiest part, because it touches on personal ego. Why? You have to call it a product/service even though it isn't *done* yet. You need to launch, get it out there in the wild, measure the results, and learn. This requires humility and a spirit of "let's try it."

How do I test my idea before risking too much?

You need to be okay with the fact that it *may* reflect poorly on you. I get that. But so what? Value progress over perfection.

> *Example:* You want to start a clothing company. Design and make some initial products in small batches. Find a local flea market where you can easily and affordably get a booth. Set up your products and try to sell them. See what happens.

Bottom Line
Innovative people (and companies) are ones that can tolerate (not kill) and actively develop half-baked ideas into valuable ones. It is hard work, and it involves setbacks. But the MVP approach is proven to produce better outcomes. Try it.

How do I make sure I'm building something valuable?
(Exit Strategy)

4

How do I make sure I'm building something valuable?

Planning for the end at the start probably gives some a weird feeling. We like the visual of "riding off into the sunset" much more because the ending is beyond some undetermined horizon. We avoid thinking about the end. But the truth is, you will want to be done with this business or organization you're starting at some point. When that point comes, will you have a path to transition away?

Most business owners do not plan for the exit up front. They build a business that is successful but intensely dependent on them, even to an unhealthy degree. When it comes time to step away, they can't, or won't, or shouldn't to protect what they've built. They've failed to build a strong set of assets in the business that can be valued and sold to another owner—and harvested when the current owner is done.

Tech startups don't have this problem, because they often require venture capital. Investors force the formulation of an exit plan to ensure there will be a day when they can cash in on their investment. Equity must translate to real money at some point, and there needs to be a strategy to achieve that. Spend any length of time around tech startup founders, and you will surely hear about "exits." While the idea of building something to sell (or leave) might feel repulsive in the founding phase, it is essential to achieving what you ultimately want—freedom.

How do I make sure I'm building something valuable?

Tech Startup Term: "Exit Strategy"

Startup for Everyone **Translation:** An articulated plan to build objective value in your business that can grow sustainably beyond the founding team.

Imagine you are building a house. This has been a dream for you. In order to maximize your enjoyment, you design it to fit your every wish and desire.

- You love golf, so you build a putting green in the living room
- Your fireplace is the shape of a guitar, because you love rock music
- The exterior siding is a bright peach color, because you grew up in Georgia

This house will give you immense enjoyment while you live in it—designed to fit your wants, needs, and style perfectly. But then, you decide you'd like to move across the country to pursue a new opportunity. It is time to sell. Should be no problem, right? You know the answer.

A crucial concept in real estate is "resale value." Conventional wisdom tells us that having stone countertops in the kitchen, upgraded bathrooms, and a well-kept lawn all increase the resale value of your home. Such features ensure that when the time comes to sell, your house will appeal to the widest variety of buyers—ultimately increasing its objective value. Unfortunately, many founders do not think this way about their business in the startup phase.

Some founders will say, "I don't care. I'm building this business for me." Like the house, that's great while you're running it, but not so great when you're ready to be done. How will you ever be able to leave?

The answer: Build something objectively valuable from the start.

You will not have time to think about this later. You'll be busy running your business. If selling the business is the goal, your only chance of transitioning to a new owner is that they can buy it *from* you and not *with* you. It is critical that you think about your exit strategy at your company's formation. You will be surprised at how clarifying it is to define what victory looks like well in advance. It impacts your vision, strategy, and decisions in significant ways.

Do you want to sell the business at a certain point to pursue another dream? Do you want to build a family business that can be passed down to future generations? Do you want to mentor young leaders in your community to take over the helm when you're done and coach them into your retirement? These are all great options. Define what "success" looks like to you.

The founders who are able to transition successfully out of their businesses have typically not done so by accident. They've made small decisions along the way, all with the mindset of building assets within the business that are valuable with or without them. Examples include real estate, customer lists, intellectual property, recurring revenue subscriptions, long-term contracts, a strong management team, etc. New potential owners see value in those things, and this perceived value creates a path for the previous owner to make a profitable transition to the next season of his or her life.

Bottom Line

This exercise forces you to think beyond yourself. It also gives a sense of urgency to creating a business that can be healthy and thriving independent of your involvement. You will want to spend less time on, or move on from, this business at some point in the future. As the saying goes, "The best time to plant an oak is 20 years ago." Build objective value from the start, and you'll have options when you want them.

How do I set up the business entity correctly?
(Incorporation)

5

How do I set up the business entity correctly?

A blank page with a blinking cursor is typically the scariest part of any writing process. There is so much left to do. Typing the first word feels like a Herculean effort. The same is often true for new founders when they are considering how they should set up the legal entity for their business. The task feels expensive, complicated, and riddled with legal language—which unfortunately creates artificial barriers to action.

It is true—there are a lot of decisions that need to be made to set up your business correctly. And the consequences of those decisions can have significant implications on your business's ability to grow in an organized, productive way. However, setting up your entity doesn't need to be expensive or complicated. There are good, straightforward answers to many of the questions that inexperienced founders have—but the key is to ask them in the right order and one at a time.

Tech startups have a more homogenous set of objectives than most industries. The standard mandate for a tech startup founder is to build something that works, win early customers, raise multiple rounds of venture capital to scale, and then sell the business within 5–10 years. There are exceptions of course, but the rule is universally well-known. Because of this shared objective, much of the advice in

How do I set up the business entity correctly?

tech startups lacks nuance that is important for everyone else who is starting stuff.

Tech Startup Term: "Incorporation"

Startup for Everyone **Definition:** The type of company you decide to form, and its implications for the owners.

Let's start with the basics. *Why do you need a legal entity for your business?* It is a good question that many advisors skip over but shouldn't. Understanding the value helps you stay motivated on what can otherwise feel like busy work. Having a legal entity for your business provides:

1. **Separation.** You can formally separate your personal finances from the business finances. This helps you maximize your tax deductions, simplify accounting work, and have clear visibility into how the *business* is doing.

2. **A Shield.** You create a shield of legal protection between you personally and the business activities. For example, if there is a legal claim against your business and you lose, the business will be penalized (not your family).

3. **Credibility.** Customers want to know that they are hiring a professional who is organized. Writing a check to you personally feels different than writing a check to your company. It matters, even if people say it doesn't.

4. **Path to Partnerships.** You are likely going to want the option to bring in co-owners to help you operate and grow the business, or investors who can help you fund it. A legal entity is the only way to facilitate that possibility.

Without digressing too far into legal advice (I'm not a lawyer), I want to prepare you with some inputs that will help you have a productive conversation with a lawyer on "incorporation" (the formation of your legal entity). Well thought-out inputs can help set up the right business structure to achieve your goals.

To keep it simple, the two most popular entity structures for businesses are C-Corp and LLC (Limited Liability Company). There are other variations, but I'll let your accountant and lawyer bore you with those. Answering the three questions below will likely lead you to a clear answer on which entity to form, and where to form it.

1. **Do you want to keep personal and business taxes as separate as possible?** C-Corps treat the business operations as totally separate from the business owners. Consequently, C-Corps file their own distinct business tax returns apart from their owners. LLCs, on the other hand, are most often used as "pass throughs," which means that business profits can be recorded on a personal tax return as long as there is only one owner, saving on tax prep costs. This approach does, however, intermingle personal and business more directly.
2. **Do you want or need to raise money from investors?** You can raise money into your business using an LLC or C-Corp. However, in a C-Corp, you have more flexibility as to the kinds of ownership you can sell to prospective investors. Tech startups often use C-Corps so they can use this flexibility and raise multiple rounds of investment. For most non-tech businesses, that flexibility is overkill and an LLC (with one or two investors) helps keep it simple.
3. **Do you envision your business operating locally only, or beyond?** New entities are formed through state governments, so your LLC or C-Corp must pick a home state (the technical term is "domicile"). If your business will operate primarily out of the state in which you live, then it is cheapest and easiest to form your business in that state. However, if there is a possibility

How do I set up the business entity correctly?

that you might set up multiple locations throughout the country eventually, then you should consider forming your company in a state with the most advantageous business laws (which is traditionally a state like Delaware).

Bottom Line
Forming your entity is a very tactical part of starting your business, but it has important implications. The last thing you'll want to do a year or two from now is address past mistakes in formation. You won't have time for that. Answer the questions above, talk with a lawyer or incorporation service (like Incorporate.com), and form the entity that makes the most sense. Once you do, you'll have the protection, credibility, and flexibility you need to build something great.

DESIGN

Create a business that will accomplish your goals
and also solve a problem for people.

How do I build the right founding team?
(Hacker, Hustler, Hipster)

6

How do I build the right founding team?

You have likely heard the classic dad-saying, "teamwork makes the dream work." As cheesy as that sounds, it is true. Your idea could be the best idea in the world, but if you don't have the right team to execute, the vision will never be realized. Unfortunately, our culture tends to idolize the leader/CEO, but the best businesses and organizations today had great teams at the beginning that were a key ingredient to success.

So how do you build the right team at the start? Who needs to be involved *and* why? These questions have plagued founders for generations. From my experience, first-time founders (I've been there) typically do one of a few things.

1. *Do it all myself.* Doing it yourself is noble and feels frugal—and may be necessary very early on. At some point, though, you are going to need to complement your weaknesses (you have them) in order to be successful. The business will stall if you don't.
2. *Invite my friends.* Friends can absolutely be co-founders. But just because someone is your friend doesn't mean he or she will be a good business partner. "We like each other" is not a good enough reason to go into business together.

How do I build the right founding team?

3. *Lean (too far) into experts.* Especially when founders are unsure of themselves, they tend to overcompensate for their insecurity by finding industry experts to join their team. This can be good in a lot of ways (experience is valuable), but it can also stunt new thinking.
4. *Overbuild.* Designing/building a team too big too soon can majorly backfire. Having a CEO, COO, CMO, CTO, C(X)O, and so on right from the start will result in disorganization and a lot of disappointed people. It is also expensive.

Tech startups have been wrestling with the team issue in an accelerated fashion. Things move so fast in that space that founders are often forced to make a decision quickly and pick one of the four paths above (all with flaws). Paul Graham, a successful tech startup founder and well-known tech investor, co-founded an annual invite-only program called Y-Combinator that receives applications from tech startups around the world, picks the top ten, and then invests money and time in each company to develop their idea. It is one of the best of its kind. Paul saw founders wrestling with the "who should be on my founding team?" question and came up with an approach (based on research and experience) that has become common practice in the tech startup world.

Tech Startup Term: "Hacker, Hustler, Hipster"

Startup for Everyone **Translation:** You need a product person, a sales/operations person, and a design/marketing person.

Before you get overwhelmed and quit, please hear me say that you *do not* need each one of these people or else you are doomed to fail. As with everything, there are always exceptions to the rule. You may be a team of one—and that is okay. For a while, you might need to play all three roles. However, research has shown that two to three founders with this complementary skill set gives a business the greatest likelihood of success.

Here are the roles.

1. **Hacker.** You need someone who is obsessed with the product or service. He or she cares about every little detail. This is the engineer, the artist, the manufacturer, the inventor, or the craftsman. This is the person who makes or delivers what the customers are buying. Hackers are most energized and satisfied when they are working on or delivering the "thing."
2. **Hustler.** You need someone who loves *running* the business and selling the product. Like, L-O-V-E loves it. This is the operator, the salesperson, the financial leader, and the one who makes sure stuff gets done. Hustlers spend their time writing proposals, forming partnerships, doing sales calls, dealing with lawyers and accountants, building spreadsheets, etc. They are most energized when they are selling the product or building the *business*.
3. **Hipster.** You need someone who is obsessed with attracting customers to the brand. This is the person who geeks out when talking to customers about what they *really* want. He or she is the designer, the packager, the creative, and the marketer. This person also probably dresses the coolest! Hipsters make sure customers resonate with what you're offering and are compelled to seek you out. They are most energized when they are thinking/working on your brand.

Bottom Line

Dig into the founding story of any great company you recognize, and you will find that the founding team had a mixture of these three roles. If you have two hackers (product people) and one designer, you'll make incredible product but struggle to sell or scale. If you have two hustlers (sales and operations people) and no hacker, you'll create a lot of buzz and customers, but your product will disappoint. Having gaps in your team today is okay but just be aware of where you are weakest and plan to close those gaps. Bring the right team together—and it feels like magic. Remember, teamwork makes the dream work.

How do I divide up ownership among co-founders?
(Vesting & Cliffs)

7

How do I divide up ownership among co-founders?

Dividing the equity of a new startup business among co-founders is awkward. It forces each person to objectively (and subjectively) evaluate their contributions to the idea or to the effort in building it out, or the importance of the skills they presumably bring to the table. In addition, this process becomes increasingly complex when startup teams are made up of people who already have careers with different implied sacrifices in joining the startup (previous salaries, equity in other businesses, etc.). This doesn't get easier when you are friends—or worse, family.

Typically, founder teams (incorrectly) solve this dilemma in one of four ways:

1. **The "Even Split."** They avoid the awkwardness and just divide ownership equally—50/50 or 30/30/30.
2. **The "Power Posture."** They have uncomfortable, even contentious arguments about what each of them deserves—usually unsuccessfully.
3. **The "Passive Delay."** They don't talk about it and hope to resolve it later.
4. **The "Formula Wizard."** They develop an overcomplicated calculation of who did what, when, and with whom to determine percentage ownership.

How do I divide up ownership among co-founders?

No one has to tell you that your conclusion on this matter is important. It has implications on decision control, tax liabilities, and financial gain through profits or an eventual sale of the business. This dilemma has existed for decades for new businesses, but the onslaught of new tech startups in the last 20 years has exaggerated the need for more discipline in how to determine what is *fair*. All the above options are flawed in one way or another, but what if you could **take the best of all of them for a perfect solution?**

Tech Startup Term: "Vesting & Cliffs"

Startup for Everyone **Translation:** Making your best guess about equity ownership at the beginning but then adjusting its "fairness" based on measurable work and time at the company.

There is always the risk that you are dealing with selfish jerks. But chances are much higher that your co-founders want to do what is fair for everyone involved. **Here are some examples of what would NOT be fair:**

- The equity is divided among co-founders, and then two months later one person leaves and keeps the equity even though he or she has moved on.
- Three founders divide the company evenly, but two of the founders take on 90%+ of the work and responsibilities and equity remains the same.
- Someone has been working on an idea for years, and then the co-founder bops along and wants to join and gets an equal share of the company.
- Both co-founders are working the same number of hours with the same equity, but one founder has the burden of CEO-like responsibilities and the other is doing much simpler tasks.

These all end in the same way: disagreement and disenfranchisement. **A common reason companies fail is because of founder fallout**—often on this topic in particular. So how do you get it right?

Let's say Jill and Caroline start a business. Jill had the idea and built the business plan, and then invited Caroline to join her because of the latter's industry expertise and experience building a startup.

Step 1: *Divide the equity objectively.* The general rule of thumb is to divide contributions by founders into two buckets: 1) **Idea—60%** (the original idea and business plan), 2) **Expertise—40%** (expertise to make the idea a reality). The two determine that Jill has 60% (remember, she created business plan) and Caroline (with the industry expertise) has 40%.

Step 2: *Establish a vesting schedule.* Jill and Caroline set up a vesting schedule, which means if they both commit to the business as agreed upon, they earn a quarter of their equity after every six months. If Jill takes a different job after one year and leaves Caroline to run the business, the equity split would change. Because it has been one year (two six-month periods), Jill will have vested 30% of the company (and now keeps that), but Caroline retains 70% (her original 40% plus Jill's 30% she is forfeiting) because she is sticking it out—**making her the new majority shareholder.**

Step 3: *Build in a cliff.* Life is full of unexpected twists and turns, and Jill and Caroline want to build that into their arrangement. They agree that if either one of them leaves the company in the first six months, that person forfeits all her equity to the other founder. **This is a "cliff," which keeps things fair and cordial for both Jill and Caroline in case of a quick change of mind.** If Jill leaves quickly, Caroline will then have 100% of the company and the freedom to

How do I divide up ownership among co-founders?

run it how she'd like. And Jill doesn't feel guilty for leaving the company after three months for a better opportunity.

Bottom Line
No one is a fortune-teller, and many founders fall prey to trying to cement in ownership structures WAY before they know how the facts will unfold. Using tools like vesting and cliffs ensures that ownership structure is matched with performance and contribution—preventing feelings of frustration. Equity ownership only has value if the company is successful and figuring this element out wisely on the front end pays off by allowing the founders to focus on what really matters—customers.

How do I raise money when I don't know what my business is worth?
(Convertible Debt)

8

How do I raise money when I don't know what my business is worth?

The TV Show *Shark Tank* has popularized the interaction between startup founders and investors. The problem is that most pitches start with, "Hi, my name is [Name]. I'm the founder of [Company] and I'm looking to raise [cash amount] for [percentage] of my company." This is straightforward, it seems, and sets expectations right away. The sharks write those numbers down in their notebooks. But even after a well-rehearsed pitch, the sharks and founders then often spend a lot of time haggling over just how much the company is worth. Sounds fun, doesn't it?

It's not, and it is also intimidating to most people, who feel like they just have a good idea that they want to see come into being. They don't want to be grilled by an investor on valuation because they don't know how in the world, they would come up with a number that made sense given all the variables in play. You might feel this way, and you are not alone. Many tech startups, especially in the early stages where so much is yet to be defined, do NOT try to value their businesses and raise money like they do on *Shark Tank*.

Tech Startup Term: "Convertible Debt"

How do I raise money when I don't know what my business is worth?

***Startup for Everyone* Translation:** A loan that has the option of becoming ownership in the company at a later date.

In the early stages of building a business, you have an idea and some initial plans of how you could turn that idea into something. You have no data, no sales, no reviews, and no customers. You are still developing the proof points in your concept. Your job as a founder is to do everything you can to obtain more information, maybe get some sales, and build out some validation without the need for money from investors. Often, you can build your business or organization without having to raise any external money at all.

However, there typically is a point where raising money from investors/partners is the right move to take your business to the next level. This point often occurs when the business is still at a relatively early stage, and the data, sales, customers, etc. are still too unknown to accurately value the company. Most of the time founders overvalue their business and investors undervalue it. Taking the *Shark Tank* approach would be a disaster.

As this valuation problem became even more of a reality with early stage tech companies, investors and founders innovated their way out of this dilemma through a new kind of investment method called "Convertible Debt." The way Convertible Debt works is that someone can invest money into your company without having to determine how much ownership that investment is worth. The investment starts as a traditional loan. Then—here is the "Convertible" part—that investor would have the option to convert the balance of that loan into a percentage of ownership in the company at a point when you have a lot more information.

Simple Example:

- A founder is given a loan for $50,000, 10% interest, 5-year term.
- The founder agrees to make the loan "convertible" within the loan term.
- Two years pass, and the founder owes ~$32,000 on the loan (because he or she has made some payments for two years) with three years left on the loan term.
- The investor and the founder mutually decide to convert the loan to equity (ownership).
- Based on two years of sales and projections, the founder values the business at $200,000.
- The founder agrees to convert the $32,000 balance to 16% ownership (32,000/200,000).
- The loan is no longer a liability of the company, and no more payments are made.
- This arrangement can become more complex if the founder raises more money from other investors later on. In that case, the original investor (who made the convertible debt loan) would get a discount so that his or her loan balance converts to equity at a lower valuation than that of the new investor. There are some technical terms and explanations, but I'll spare you. Any good business lawyer could walk you through the specifics.

This is a powerful way to raise money effectively and efficiently at early stages.

Top 2 benefits to founders:

1. Avoid negotiating ownership and/or value of the company with investors at an early stage.
2. Raise cash in the short term with an option to eliminate the loan payment in the long term.

How do I raise money when I don't know what my business is worth?

Top 2 benefits to investors:

1. Mitigate risk by earning interest on cash invested with an option to convert to equity upon success of the business.
2. Gain an advantage as an early investor to convert to equity at a discount compared to later investors.

Bottom Line

There is a lot of good content out there to explain this concept in more detail. Search the Internet, talk to some experts, and decide if this option is right for you. Getting an investor to buy into your vision enough to put in money is hard enough, so keep the terms simple and mutually beneficial. Convertible debt is one option to get you there.

How do I win customers when I'm new and unproven?
(Alpha & Beta)

9

How do I win customers when I'm new and unproven?

When you start something, you feel like a fake. It is a hard feeling to avoid—even if you have experience. All of your competitors are bigger, more credible, and have momentum. This reality hits you hard when you first start selling and a customer asks, "So, what other customers do you have?" You know the answer (they likely do, too), but it is a shameful experience to say "none." The good news is that any business you love started with no customers. Apple, Ford, and Patagonia all began as new ideas that were unproven, untested, and void of a track record. The founders of those companies likely also felt like imposters.

You have a *choice* in how to deal with this dynamic.

- Option 1: **Pretend** like you are more established than you actually are.
- Option 2: **Rely** only on your past experience before starting this business.
- Option 3: **Invite** people honestly into *your* journey.

Pretending and relying too heavily on the past exaggerates the feeling of being a fake. Instead, inviting people into your journey as a new business gives freedom, transparency, and a collaborative spirit that will give you surprising confidence. So how do you do it?

How do I win customers when I'm new and unproven?

Digital technology offers the ability for new tech startups to create early working versions of products quickly. They can offer users the opportunity to try the roughest version of their product, give honest feedback, watch the company make improvements, and then try new versions. Over the years, this has become a more standard and accepted practice for overcoming the "we're new and unproven" dilemma. As a result, when these companies are ready to launch their real product, they already have a proven track record of engaging with real customers. **Every business, tech and non-tech, can benefit from this approach.**

Tech Startup Term: Alpha & Beta Testing

Startup for Everyone **Translation:** Creating early versions of your product that can be tested in a transparent, collaborative way that helps establish confidence.

You need to call it what it is at the beginning of your new business. When a prospective customer asks, "Do you have other customers?" the answer can be, "Nope! But I want to invite you into a small group of early customers to test my offering at a discounted rate, and in return, I'll ask for your feedback on how I can improve going forward." You just started an **Alpha** test. While the word sounds technical (that is its origin), it establishes a safe environment to say that you are still figuring out what you are doing.

What makes a good Alpha test?

- **Product/Offering.** You need to create the simplest version of your product or offering that will still give you the feedback you need to validate your most critical assumptions. Don't try to over-impress—it is okay if there are rough edges or some mistakes.
- **Charge Money.** Tech companies can do stuff for free. You *can* do that, but that is not a requirement. Instead of offer-

- ing your product or service for free, offer it at a discount or give early customers preferred pricing going forward. Some companies have even given Alpha customers notoriety or recognition through plaques on the wall or by calling them "Pioneers."
- **Test Everything.** Don't pretend to have your act together or to know more than you do. Test your pricing, your communication cadence, your logo, your invoicing process, and your product itself. Try to answer the question: "When this is a real customer, will I be proud of my whole business?"
- **Make it Exclusive.** People like to be invited into something special. Make your Alpha group of testers a limited number. Say, "I'm looking for ten people to join a private testing group on my new business. It comes with X, Y, and Z benefits." Ideally, you can say, "I already have three customers signed up."
- **Define a Timeframe.** Alpha tests shouldn't last forever—there should be a deadline that seems close. In general, these tests should last more than a week but less than 3 months. Try to estimate the time you'll need to gather information from this group and then stop the test, thank your Alpha customers, and announce the start date of your next test—the **Beta test.**

Beta comes after Alpha, as you know, and is essentially the same thing but with a larger group and a more proven product. Do an Alpha. Do a Beta. And then launch—even if you don't feel ready! You have to at some point, but now you'll have a track record with real customers.

Bottom Line

You are not a fake. You are not an imposter. You just haven't tried yet. Once you do, you'll become more confident and committed. And before long, you'll love answering questions about your customer list.

How do I determine the right pricing?
(Value Metric)

10

How do I determine the right pricing?

Pricing is usually a sensitive topic for founders. It becomes the ultimate measure of worth for what they create or provide, which makes it feel evaluative and personal. The spectrum of what founders think of themselves or their product is wide. As a result, some founders are not confident enough to charge what they are worth. Other founders price themselves ambitiously but unrealistically high.

While pricing is both an art and a science, the decision can devolve into a hornet's nest of tension and frustration when emotions are involved. Making a rational, thoughtful, and market-driven decision about pricing is the most solid path to an answer that everyone can feel good about. It also helps your business work. So how do you get there?

In the purest sense, pricing is a game of give-and-take between a business and its customers. It is the conventional matchmaking of supply (what you make) and demand (what people will pay for it). Eventually, the two parties settle on a number that seems fair and mutually beneficial. The key is to find this answer quickly, because an incorrectly priced product can be a fatal flaw.

Tech startups have driven significant pricing innovation over the past decade. From movie rental (like Netflix) to public auctions (like eBay), and from fashion shopping (like StitchFix or Trunk Club) to group chat (like Slack) or to mental health (like HeadSpace), we've

How do I determine the right pricing?

seen massive evolutions in how we pay for products and services. The new methods feel better and fairer to customers, and steadier for businesses. Why? These companies have helped push pricing closer to the most fundamental driver of the business/customer exchange: value.

Tech Startup Term: "Value Metric"

Startup for Everyone Translation: The benefit your customer cares about most that will play the most significant role in her/his willingness to pay you.

There are many different ways to set a price. I am not going to digress into teaching you pricing mechanics—that is not the point of this chapter. My primary goal is to help you understand why value metrics are so important, and how they affect pricing.

A common way to determine a price is to start with the cost of the product ("it costs me $10 to make this product") and then charge a premium on top of that (for example, $5), making the final price to the customer $15. This is called "cost-plus pricing." Using this method, your business would profit $5 per product sold. Is that good? We don't know. Not until we understand the value each customer is receiving can we adequately answer whether or not this profit equation on your product is "good." And that can be done through value metrics.

Do you love yard work? Some people do, believe it or not. However, most people do not enjoy mowing their lawn. This fact explains why there are likely dozens of lawncare companies wherever you live (unless you live in the desert, of course). Lawncare is a great example of a value metric driving pricing.

A lawncare provider can likely mow the average American lawn in about 30 minutes. Take the hourly wage of the person mowing the lawn (let's say $20), divide that by two ($10), and you have the cost the lawncare company incurred to provide you a mowed lawn (not including normal operating costs). Using the same numbers as above, should they charge you $15? Is $5 a good profit?

This is where value metrics come in. Customers don't care how long it takes the lawncare company to mow the lawn. That point is irrelevant. They want a *mowed lawn* (their value metric). That is what matters most to them, and they have assigned a subjective value to not having to do it themselves. That value is likely higher than $15—so only charging $15 leaves a lot of *value* on the table. Could the lawncare company charge $100? Probably not. But they'd likely be able to charge something in between $15 and $100.

The value metric in lawn care is *mowed lawns*. The value metric for locksmiths could be *unlocked cars*. The value metric for a train is *safe arrivals*. Customers value something enough that they are willing to exchange money for it. If your product creates little to no discrete value, no one will buy it. When your price is aligned with the value the *customer receives* from your product or service, there isn't as much to negotiate or fret over.

Bottom Line
Determining your value metric demystifies and depersonalizes the pricing discussion. It is not about you, or even about what you made. The main point of discussion is the value created and what that is worth to a prospective customer. If customers can pay you equal to or less than what the product or service is worth to them, they are happy. And when they are happy, you get value in return.

DEVELOP

Set up your business in a way that mitigates risk and ensures a solid foundation for growth.

How do I not run out of money?
(Burn Rate)

11

How do I not run out of money?

You will get all kinds of advice as a founder. Some will be good; some will not. As always, the effectiveness of any advice depends on how you apply it. Many people will have opinions about your product and advise you accordingly. The next-most-popular subject about which to offer input is money.

Two of the most common bits of entrepreneurial money advice seem completely at odds with each other:

- Bit of Advice 1: "Cash is king. Guard it with your life."
- Bit of Advice 2: "You have to spend money to make money."

When you're starting something new, *both are true*—but how?

I've met many founders who are *very* proud of how frugal they've been with their startup money. They have stories of how they've stretched their dollars well beyond what would seem possible. And in the end, they fail. While frugality is a virtue, so is investment. You will not achieve your goals if you hold on to every nickel you've saved or raised. It doesn't work that way.

Tech startups (especially in Silicon Valley) often get a bad rap for raising and spending *a lot of money*. To the rest of us, it is shocking to hear how much money these startups go through while building. It makes you wonder if they are literally burning it for heat.

How do I not run out of money?

These startups are playing a different game than most small businesses. The goal is *not* to last as long as possible. The goal is to build as *fast* as possible, and that takes money. Tech startup founders need to walk a fine line between foolishness and bravery, waiting and speed, and saving and spending. Growth is *the* goal, and that is not free. While you may not be interested in spending hundreds of thousands of dollars per month, you do need to think about navigating the frugality/investment balance at the start.

Tech Startup Term: "Burn Rate"

Startup for Everyone **Translation:** The amount of money you need to invest each week/month/year before you become profitable.

Not many public companies discuss their "burn rate" with investors. That is because they are expected to be returning money back to shareholders in the form of profits. Once a business is established, making more money than is spent is a fair expectation.

In the startup phase, being profitable too early can actually be a bad sign. It signals to you, co-founders, and investors that the business has a low ceiling and has maxed out its potential. If a business has the potential to be big eventually, it often requires a period of early investment to cover costs. This is called the "burn rate," or the amount you are *investing* each week/month/year to achieve a level of scale that accomplishes your hopes for this business.

For example, let's say you decide to make homemade necklaces that you sell online. You buy just enough material to make 50 necklaces, construct them carefully, and then post some pictures and prices on Facebook. This whole process takes you a month. And you sell out, making $200 in profit.

If you are satisfied, you keep making 50 necklaces at a time and selling out, chipping off $200 in profit each month. You are making money, which is great, but right now you have a small side business, not a company. If you desire to turn this side hustle into something that would allow you to hire some employees, build a brand, make other products, and provide a stable income, you'll need to invest and accept a burn rate to get there.

This does not give startup founders the excuse to start spending money like crazy and call it investment. For example, the Herman Miller Eames chair is a beautiful piece of furniture for your office, but not an investment in your business. Every dollar should clearly link to the potential for profit and momentum. If not, don't spend it.

Back to you as a necklace maker. You spend $3,000 on a website, design a logo for $600, and spend $200 per month on social media marketing. Your $200 per month profit will not cover those costs, but that is okay. You know you'll reach more people, sell more product, and start to build momentum—eventually. The gap between what you're making now and what you need to spend to achieve a new, higher level of sales is your burn rate. Successful founders have a period of time wherein they are choosing to invest in the future.

Bottom Line

When money is tight, no one wants to spend it. Cash is still king. But it is important to grasp the concept that a business often "loses money" before it makes money. Fixating too intensely on cost savings and profitability at the beginning results in a much smaller, less valuable business in the long run. Build for what you long for, not just what you can bear today.

How do I stay in business if my first idea is failing?
(Pivot)

12

How do I stay in business if my first idea is failing?

No matter who you are, it is always hard to say, "I was wrong." You feel disappointment, discouragement, and doubt that weigh down your entrepreneurial confidence. After all, you convinced yourself, your team, your investors, and your family members on a vision that is simply not materializing as you scripted. On its current path, it appears the venture is destined for a dead end. So, what now?

It is a near certainty that founders of every kind of business or organization will encounter this humbling moment. Plans become outdated fast in a startup. As nineteenth-century military leader Helmuth von Moltke once said, "No battle plan survives contact with the enemy." Your customers aren't your enemy, but the principle still holds true. Ideas are full of false assumptions.

In fact, it is highly likely that more than 50% of your first idea is *flat-out wrong*. That statement is not meant to offend you; it is meant to prepare you. Being wrong is part of the process of building something right.

How do I stay in business if my first idea is failing?

Tech startup founders are actually rewarded for saying "I was wrong" often, because failing toward the right answer is expected. Venture capitalists will tell you that they consider founders who have not yet encountered failure as riskier investments than those who have. "What We Have Learned" is one of the most popular slides in a startup pitch deck because it demonstrates that the false assumptions have already been rooted out of the original idea. Every successful startup journey is full of adjustments, commonly called *pivots*.

Tech Startup Term: "Pivot"

Startup for Everyone **Translation:** Making a change that leverages what you have already built but points your business in a new, more valuable direction.

Brands we all recognize today because of their success often started off as something *very* different.

- *YouTube* began as a dating service.
- *Wrigley* began as a baking powder company.
- *Slack* began as a video game.
- *Suzuki* began as a sewing machine manufacturer.
- *Groupon* began as a platform for social movements.

Some of these origin stories might seem random. How does one start by selling baking powder and end up with chewing gum as the staple product, translating to billions of dollars in annual sales?

Mr. Wrigley's first business idea was to sell household products (like soap and baking powder) to drug and grocery stores. Wrigley also had a knack for marketing, so he added a piece of chewing gum attached to the product in the same way toys accompany McDonald's Happy Meals. People came to love the chewing gum so much that they bought soap just to chew it. Wrigley's chomping empire developed from an unexpected place.

Many founders get too attached to their original vision. They spent so much time working on, planning for, and designing around a concept that isn't being met with promise. They get frustrated with customers or partners because they "don't get it." And as a result, they often miss opportunities to build the business that is being demanded by the market. Imagine if Mr. Wrigley ignored the popularity of his gum just because that wasn't his original idea.

Founders need to be willing to change, to pivot their business to what will work. It is, however, important to understand that pivoting is not the same as abandoning everything you have built thus far. Pivoting is more like repositioning.

Imagine a basketball player holding a ball, keeping one foot planted on the ground but moving the other foot to rotate her body to face a new direction. If you look up the stories of any well-known business pivots, you will learn that the founders always leveraged the best parts/assets of their original idea, discarded the irrelevant, and then pursued the newfound direction with commitment.

When the original idea is not working as expected, here are some questions to ask yourself:

- *What has surprised you?* The best entrepreneurs are naturally curious, and therefore grow accustomed to surprises. They take risks, try new things, and expect to be continually learning. They realize that surprises are often laced with the potential for newfound wisdom.
- *What has frustrated you?* Your points of frustration might be areas where you are trying to force something that is not meant to work. Perseverance is a virtue, for sure, but it can quickly slip into foolishness if you're not careful. Your list of annoyances might be interesting inputs for pivot.
- *What are you resisting?* Momentum is everything when you are getting started. But founders who are fixated on follow-

How do I stay in business if my first idea is failing?

ing a script are often resisting the pull of the business in a new direction. If it takes effort to fend off momentum in areas you weren't expecting, pay attention.
- *What are you good at?* Skills are more transferrable than many people think. Too often founders get stuck in the "I only know this industry" trap and spin their wheels without pivoting to the unknown territory where the momentum is. Trust yourself, and your ability to learn new things.

Bottom Line
Your original plan was worth the effort. It helped you to clarify your idea, think carefully about execution, and recruit the right people to the table. It served its purpose. Now, your ability to achieve success will depend on your ability to adjust quickly and aggressively during the journey. Pivot until you find the sweet spot, and then commit and build something great.

How do I determine who my target customer should be?
(Adoption Curve)

13

How do I determine who my target customer should be?

There is a blissful moment when an idea first hits you. You believe that everyone will absolutely get it, and its existence will truly make the world a better place. That moment of bliss often quickly slips away after you start talking to people. The enthusiastic reaction you were hoping for doesn't quite transpire the way you thought. It makes you wonder, "Hmm, maybe there isn't something here after all?" Eventually, you wise up and determine that this idea *is valuable,* but it may not be relevant to everyone. You need a target customer—a specific group of people or businesses on whom to focus your efforts. But who should that "target" be?

This problem is exaggerated in tech companies because the world is their oyster. Technology is not confined by geography or even by industry. So very quickly, tech startups can find themselves boiling the ocean, promising to meet everyone's needs perfectly, and finding out that their idea just doesn't resonate with most people. In 1962, professor Everett Rogers developed a concept that addressed this issue more broadly for new, innovative ideas. Recently, it has been wholeheartedly adopted by tech startups because it gives very specific direction on whom to focus and when to focus on them as a business or organization is being built.

How do I determine who my target customer should be?

Tech Startup Term: "Adoption Curve"

***Startup for Everyone* Translation:** A way to group your potential customers into segments based on the way they typically buy/adopt stuff, informing whom to target with your idea at the start.

People react to new ideas differently. Your idea could solve a person's problem perfectly, but if his or her natural bias toward new ideas is negative, that doesn't matter. You could make the mistake of thinking that the idea is bad when in fact, it is not. Professor Rogers argues that the general population falls into one of five categories when adopting new stuff, and those categories matter immensely when trying to convince people to buy what you're selling.

Here are the five categories:

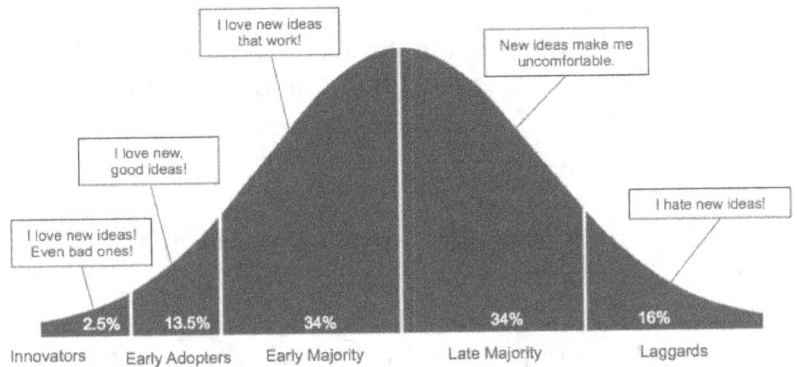

(Based on Rogers *Adoption Curve*)

Innovators (2.5% of people). Innovators love new ideas. In fact, they seek them out. They are the ones who spent $4,000 on a plasma television when that product first hit the market because it was important to them to be the first to have or try it. Innovators will often

69

try things before they even work right—and they are okay with that. Products/services they like to buy are *new and different.*

> POINT: This is your target customer at the beginning.

Early Adopters (13.5% of people). Early adopters also love new ideas, but they are a bit more conservative. They will try things before they are massively popular as long as there are some solid reviews from early users (the Innovators). They are not as sensitive to price as long as it is not ludicrous. Products/services they like to buy are *new and validated.*

> POINT: This is also your target customer at the beginning after you get some early traction.

Early Majority (34% of people). Early majority people are drawn to *good* ideas. They are indifferent to whether or not ideas are new so long as they work. If a concept or product is proven and reliable, they are on board. This group is really important because if you win them over, your business is bound to take off. Products/services they like to buy are *good and proven.*

> POINT: This is your target customer once you have success stories and client testimonials.

Late Majority (34% of people). The late majority is usually hesitant and skeptical of new ideas from the start. Even if the product totally solves their problem, they need to be convinced to change. They typically buy on price and functionality and will want to see other options before deciding. Products/services they like to buy are *established and generate obvious value.*

> POINT: This is your target customer further down the line. They typically come to you when they are ready.

How do I determine who my target customer should be?

Laggards (16% of people). Laggards do not like anything new—at all. If they could still buy and use a rotary phone, they absolutely would. They oppose new ideas and will only adopt them if they have no other choice. They like things the way they are. Change is annoying to them. Products/services they like to buy are *stuff they are used to.*

> POINT: This is NOT your customer. That's okay. Don't let their opinions discourage you.

Bottom Line
Seemingly old-fashioned companies can have an Innovator as a decision maker. They might surprise you how fast they make decisions. New, progressive companies that you would think to be innovative can have a Late Majority individual as a decision maker – making it hard to gain buy-in. It is about people. If you try to sell to Late Majority and Laggards at the beginning, you'll hit a wall. Don't try. Define your Innovators and Early Majority. What do they want? How do they think? What would make them say yes? Tap into that, build an experience around them, and then launch with them. They will help you get to the next category and beyond.

How do I avoid trying to be everything to everyone?
(Personas)

14

How do I avoid trying to be everything to everyone?

New founders are especially impressionable to customer feedback—for good reason. They want what they are doing to resonate with people. For the most part, this impressionability is a great thing, as it drives regular iteration on your product or service to ensure that it solves an important problem.

At first, this feedback comes in manageable doses and can be applied quickly. The process feels good, and people are happy with your responsiveness. But as the number of customers starts to grow, the quantity and diversity of feedback becomes unmanageable. It becomes confusing, in fact. In some cases, one set of customers wants something that is in direct conflict with another set.

Highly motivated founders decide to push through this conflict and confusion, going down the "be everything to everyone" path to appease every customer's wish. Eventually, they discover this effort is a dead end of impossibly high expectations and insufficient delivery on promises. The founder tires of people-pleasing and becomes frustrated with the chaos. How do *you* avoid this perpetual struggle?

How do I avoid trying to be everything to everyone?

This problem is especially acute in digital technology. There are no *physical* limitations to what a digital product can do. After all, it is just a little bit of code, right? This presents a problem. Theoretically, any bit of feedback a digital startup receives could be applied—and *should* be applied—in the mind of the customer. As a result, tech startups are often overwhelmed with requests, and it becomes harder to see a clear path forward to success. Many have found it especially helpful to create discrete segments of their customer base, often in the form of fictional characters or "Personas," to help parse through the feedback and make disciplined decisions about priorities.

Tech Startup Term: "Personas"

***Startup for Everyone* Translation:** Creating highly specific descriptions of the types of customers you have that help drive decisions on prioritization.

As the customer input mounts, too many founders create a "super customer." This super customer is the culmination of all possible desires—everything anyone has ever wanted in your product. They have monstrous expectations that oftentimes contradict each other. They want it cozier, but roomier. They want it smaller, but more substantial. They want it cheaper, but more luxurious. At some point, you find yourself paralyzed and unable to move forward.

Good news! The super customer doesn't exist. No one has all those demands all at once. The super customer is often a composition of all the multiple personalities that make up your customer base, each of which comes from a very different perspective, and with a different set of problems to solve. Tech startups have found it especially helpful to use fictional names to represent each customer segment. That way, when they discuss feedback, they can ask: "Which customer is this for?"

Let's use the example of a bicycle shop. Instead of thinking of their customers as one complex entity of expectations, the shop owners decide to break these expectations down into four distinct fictional personas: Shelly, Karen, Jim, Angelica, and Roy. Let's meet them.

Shelly: An avid cyclist for 20+ years. Cares very much about quality, brand, and performance. Has very high demands for service work. Extremely loyal to her bike shop if she trusts and has a relationship with the owner.

Karen: An avid cyclist for 20+ years. Cares very much about quality, brand, and performance. Has very high demands for service work. Extremely loyal to her bike shop if she trusts and has a relationship with the owner.

Jim: A committed bike commuter, who rode his bike to work before it was cool to do so. Cares about comfort, durability, and storage options. Rides his bike in difficult conditions, so has a lot of wear and tear he needs help with.

Angelica: An active, 40-year-old woman with three kids. Maintains a healthy and busy lifestyle, and values outdoor activities. Cares less about brand, and more about affordability. Wants reliable expertise, and good customer service.

Roy: A local business owner who wants to support other small business owners. Doesn't know anything about bikes and doesn't really care to. He wants the "most popular bike" at a cheap price. Filling a need, and that's it.

Now, imagine combining all of these personalities into one monstrous customer. That customer would be impossible to please! Instead, breaking these demands into four distinct personas helps you understand context when you are processing customer feedback.

How do I avoid trying to be everything to everyone?

Did Roy say that the shop feels too small, or did Shelly? Because depending on who said it, it means two very different things. This structure also helps you evaluate new ideas (not just customer feedback). As you run through the potential of a new idea, you might say: "What would Angelica think about this? What about Jim? And what about Shelly?"

These aren't real people, but it doesn't matter. These four fictitious individuals represent your customer base, are memorably distinct, and will help you sift through feedback and understand the context. As a result, you can determine priorities swiftly and quiet the noise.

Bottom Line
Founders have so much pulling at their attention, and confusion in the area of customer feedback can cause a lot of unhealthy and unnecessary stress. Drawing clear lines around the customer base gives you freedom to think with poise and conviction. It also empowers you to lead your team well and invokes empathy for people (even if they are fake) instead of fear. Over time, you might even find ways to meet all your customers right where they are, and with what they need—at scale.

How do I stay organized and build something solid?
(Technical Debt)

15

How do I stay organized and build something solid?

Many founders have the best intentions to stay organized when they start something new. They might even buy a planner and color-coded sticky notes or design a sophisticated checklist system. They look at other disheveled business owners and convince themselves they can do much better. However, any experienced founder will tell you that the unpredictable reality and pace of a new business quickly disrupts any sincere effort to stay organized.

In a new business, change is a constant. The impacts of each new change begin to compound exponentially. For example, the product costs more to make than you thought it would, so you change the design. A customer gives you feedback you didn't expect, so you change your sales approach. An employee whom you trust leaves you unexpectedly, so you have more responsibility on your plate. You sign a contract that is well beyond your capabilities, so you scramble to put the pieces in place. Now, you have a different product, a different approach, more responsibilities, and a brand-new contract to deliver under pressure. Things get messy.

It is easy to assume that the perceived mess is a result of bad decisions, poor business acumen, or laziness. But oftentimes messy businesses are messy because they are successful. Customers want the

How do I stay organized and build something solid?

product, the brand is resonating, and there just isn't enough time to stay organized. (It is easy to keep things organized when no one wants what you sell). In growing tech startups, the pace of frequent changes in response to growing demand creates too many "we'll fix that later" moments, resulting in increasingly messy code. Messy code is fine in the short term but can eventually create an unstable and irreparable product in the long term.

Tech Startup Term: "Technical Debt"

***Startup for Everyone* Term**: The collection of "we'll fix that later" decisions that must be cleaned up in order to avoid major issues later on.

You might have heard the expression that leading a new business is like "building a plane while you're flying it." The analogy perfectly depicts what it feels like when someone points out an obvious flaw in what you are doing, and you're forced to say, "I know, I know. I just haven't gotten to that yet." New founders grow accustomed to feeling like they are surrounded by duct tape and extension cords, trying to keep the business (and themselves) alive. While living this way can be a thrill at the beginning, it is not sustainable. Eventually, the duct tape decisions will lose hold, and the "we'll only do this one time" extension cords will tangle uncontrollably.

It is not just new founders who deal with this issue. Have you ever wondered why insurance companies still require faxed applications? Or why many airline ticketing systems look like they were built in the 90's? Or have you witnessed a restaurant still using written order forms? These are all examples of unkept technical debt.

Why is this a big deal? A server taking orders on notepads in messy handwriting can be endearing in your favorite local restaurant. But what happens when that restaurant tries to double its dining space, which doubles the hand-scribbled notes? Predictably, a new cook spills a pot of marinara sauce all over a large stack of pending orders. What then?

Mistakes happen in every business—it is a certainty. Technical debt amplifies simple mistakes into catastrophes because past unaddressed flaws create a domino effect. Tech startup product teams have implemented several disciplines to manage technical debt and avoid catastrophes.

1. **Log.** When you make a decision that is effective in the moment, but you know will need to be fixed later, *write it down*. Keep an ongoing list.
2. **Evaluate.** Review this list with your team and determine the 1) relevance, 2) urgency, 3) effort needed to resolve the issue. Give each one a score.
3. **Envision.** Look ahead at your future plans and assess which set of issues will be most problematic to fulfilling your goals.
4. **Schedule.** Define a time to reduce your debt by addressing the most relevant, urgent, and potentially problematic issues.
5. **Repeat.** Continue to address "we'll fix it later" issues on a regular basis, thus ensuring you build toward a business that is solid and mistake resilient.

Bottom Line

The concept of technical debt doesn't just apply to technology businesses. It is an essential concept to understand as an entrepreneur of any kind. You are likely making decisions every day that are disguised shortcuts. You know that they will catch up to you eventually, so don't ignore them. Build intentional time into your monthly, quarterly, and annual calendar to go back and clean up the shortcuts. Yes, this may force you to slow down, but it will eventually help you operate successfully at high speeds.

DRIVE

Lead your business to its full potential in a way that is sustainable.

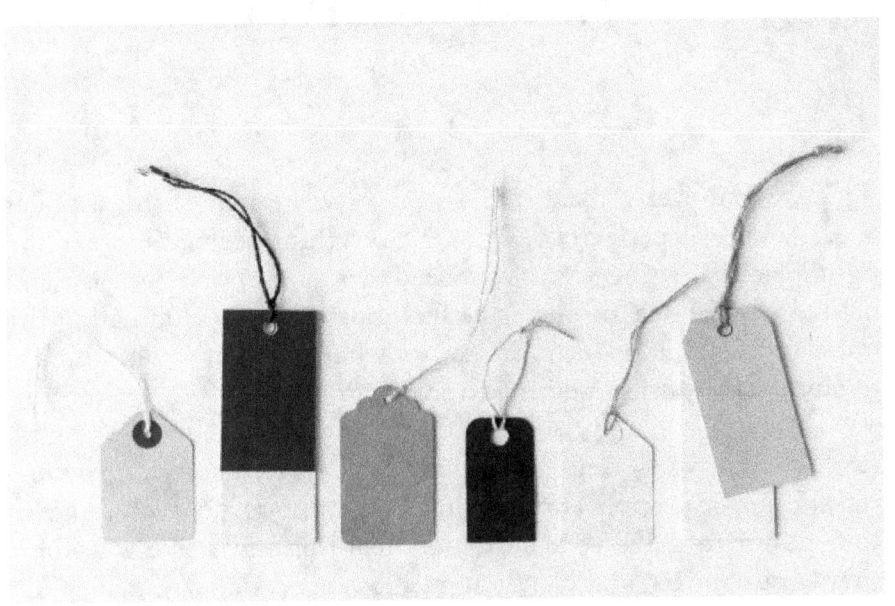

How do I know the right way to sell my product?
(A/B Testing)

16

How do I know the right way to sell my product/service?

Have you ever walked into a store or visited a website that felt like it was perfectly designed? Everything seemed to be in the right place? Getting what you needed was surprisingly easy and natural? **Good design makes us feel motivated** by eliminating the noise and helping us focus on exactly what we want to do, which is to buy, try, or learn something to solve our problem.

And whether you're selling a product in a store, a service in a conversation, or an application online, you want to do everything in your power to make your customers feel this way—like you **knew they were coming,** and you thought about every detail to make their experience ideal.

No one designs the way they sell their product perfectly out of the gate. If you do, you should play the lottery. There is always a period of trial and error when you're trying a bunch of stuff to see what works. But that **experimentation can be exhausting** because the options seem limitless and the results are all over the place. This is definitely true for tech startups, whose canvas for experimentation is especially broad. Digital technology has opened the door to more savvy ways to experiment, and those new methods have had huge impacts on the way things are sold online. Good news! You can apply these methods to the thing you are starting (whether it is online or not).

How do I know the right way to sell my product/service?

Tech Startup Term: "A/B Testing"

***Startup for Everyone* Translation:** A focused experiment wherein you test one approach vs. another over a period of time, measure the results, and then pick the best one.

In tech startups, A/B testing is a great way to move toward perfect design. This is an example of how it works:

1. **Design.** An experiment sends half of website visitors to a design that has the "BUY" button on the left (A) and the other half to a different design that has the "BUY" button on the right (B).
2. **Measure.** The experiment runs long enough to get people to try both versions, until the team feels like it is clear which location for the "BUY" button generates the most clicks.
3. **Decide.** The experiment is done. The startup moves the "BUY" button to the ideal spot (left or right), and then designs a new experiment to discover what color the button should be.

This process can be repeated over and over until the perfect design is created. You can do the same, even if you're not using a website.

A Practical Example
Imagine you are selling fencing. You know the product inside and out, and you've got all the materials ready for six appointments scheduled today. You have your pitch rehearsed and process for selling mapped out (introduce yourself, walk outside to measure the desired fenced area, discuss finishes/materials, discuss budget, propose pricing, ask for the order). The traditional approach would be to use the same order of tasks with all six customers, and hope you close some deals. But if you use the same approach every time, you may not be learning the *ideal* way for *you* to sell fencing.

An A/B test would be to split your appointments into two buckets. With three of the customers, you are going to take your traditional approach. With the other three customers, you're going to discuss budget first, finishes second, and then go and measure the fenced area last. What approach leads to more orders? Measure the results, decide on the best order of tasks, and then design a new experiment to tweak the process even further.

The Bottom Line
You don't need to know the ideal way to sell to your customers immediately when you are getting started. Here is a secret: no one knows. We're all making it up as we go. Start with a guess, and experiment from there. Using A/B testing allows you to take what feels like abstract art and make it something more understandable. Play around with it. I think you'll be surprised how fun it is, and the impact it can have on your ability to hear "yes" more often.

How do I find more customers predictably?
(Conversion Funnel)

17

How do I find more customers predictably?

Have you ever walked into a dark room and been unable to find the light switch? It is annoying, confusing, and kind of scary. sometimes. When money is tight and timelines are short, entrepreneurs (especially new ones) feel the same way about their marketing efforts. They feel like they are frantically searching for the switch that turns on a steady flow of customers to their business but can't seem to find it.

The searching turns to desperation and eventually evolves into a cadre of random, disparate efforts with little to marginal success. In many cases, these entrepreneurs throw up their hands and say, "marketing is a waste of money."

Marketing doesn't have to be a money wasting activity. It *can* be a systematic, measurable, and (most importantly) *adjustable* science – providing clear, compelling answers to what does or does not work.

In a tech startup, the pressure to prove traction right away is significant, and clearly tied to raising money (for good reason). Under the pressure of an expected pace of growth, founders have been driven to develop a new take on an old concept that (for them) meaningfully connects different marketing activities with the acquisition of

How do I find more customers predictably?

real customers (and everything in between). It has brought rigor and discipline where there was once chaos and made "What is your conversion funnel?" a common conversation among tech founders and their investors.

Tech Startup Term: "Conversion Funnel"

***Startup for Everyone* Translation:** A series of calculations that helps you understand how people make it through each step of the buying process to eventually become your customers.

For illustration, let's consider an exercise studio you just started. Success and sustainability of the business is defined by a steady group of "members," who pay monthly dues for access to regular classes. As a new studio owner, your main goal is to **attract and retain members quickly** with the limited amount of marketing dollars you have to spend. Should you do Facebook ads? Post flyers at coffee shops? Give out referral/discount codes to your friends to share? Or maybe pass them out at a public event in your community?

Let's say that there is a big public event in your community and your plan is to pass out 1,000 flyers with a "free class" promo code to attract new people to your studio. To do this well, you need to **define your conversion funnel.** Huh?

A "funnel" is something that is wide at the top and then gradually narrows toward the bottom. While everyone understands that concept (and has likely used a funnel to add fuel to a lawnmower), the actual typical approach taken by many entrepreneurs with their initial marketing is (unfortunately) a "pointy plate."

Pointy Plate Strategy: You pass out flyers and cross your fingers that it works. It looks something like this:

"Pointy Plate"

Feel familiar? It is nerve-racking. If it does work, you might not know why or if it will work again. If it doesn't, you may never try it again (but for the wrong reasons). How would a conversion funnel work differently?

Conversion Funnel

1. Define the specific steps that each potential customer takes from receiving the flyer to becoming a member (and everything in between).
2. Measure the conversion rate at each step of the process.
3. Review the conversion rates at each step and ask, "Does that seem about right? Is it low? If so, what can I do differently?"
4. Count the number of members who join (end of the funnel), total up their value, and determine whether or not the marketing effort was "worth it."

In the exercise studio example, the conversion funnel looks like this:

How do I find more customers predictably?

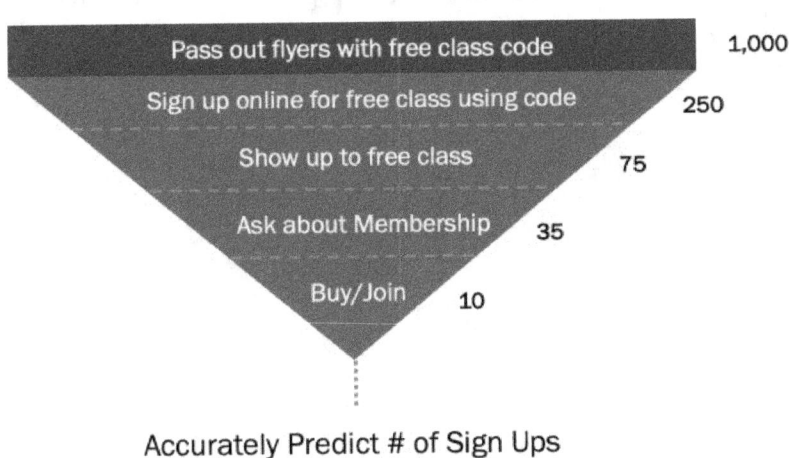

Accurately Predict # of Sign Ups
(and therefore justify the marketing investment)

The conversion funnel indicates that you passed out 1,000 flyers and generated 10 new members. If you spent $1,500 on the flyers strategy (including printing, staffing, etc.) and generated 10 new members ($500/mo. in value), then you pay back your marketing efforts in three months and generate $4,500 in additional profit (9 months X $500) for the remainder of the year.

Spend $1,500 to get $4,500 in profit. That's a good deal. And theoretically, you could pass out $2,000 worth of flyers and generate $9,000 in additional profit. It's a formula.

What is most important is that you can find ways to improve your conversion at each step of the process. For example, you could simplify the online experience of entering your code, you could train your front desk staff to have more effective conversations about membership, and so on. Thinking this way makes marketing a more systematic, predictable, and adjustable science. You know right where the light switch is.

Bottom Line

Any good businessperson will tell you that the path to success is a series of minor adjustments—tweaking, iterating, and discovering. A steady stream of new customers to your business is no different. Master your conversion funnel, master your business.

How do I ensure customers have a great experience?
(Onboarding)

18

How do I ensure customers have a great experience?

You can't have a successful business without happy customers. While that fact may seem obvious, too many founders overlook this simple truth. It is easy to get wrapped up in your product, brand, team, finances, or operational tasks and forget that the whole business goes away without customers. As Amazon founder Jeff Bezos says, "They are the only ones who give you money." Deliberate effort must be made to keep the customer front and center in *every decision*.

Happy customers are a result of a wonderfully designed experience. You could have the best product in the world, but if new customers don't know how to get the most out of it, they will stop paying you. Mayo Clinic, for example, is a hospital in Rochester, Minnesota renowned for its unparalleled patient experience. It attracts some of the most talented doctors and complex medical cases in the world. Its stellar reputation is not due to employees being especially nice or trying really hard. Mayo went beyond that, taking the time to put itself in the shoes of a patient and optimizing from that perspective.

We are all inundated these days with apps and digital tools to help improve our lives. The tech startups providing these tools have historically fallen into the "build it and they will come" trap to a startlingly high degree. The teams focused on delivering a beautiful, functional

How do I ensure customers have a great experience?

product that no one used—leading to inevitable peril. There is therefore increasing insistence for all new tech startups to think carefully about how new users can quickly find value in the product—resulting in much higher rates of retention. This realization has created the discipline of onboarding—with powerful financial results.

Tech Startup Term: "Onboarding"

***Startup for Everyone* Translation**: A precisely defined and implemented process to help new customers thoroughly enjoy your product or service.

New customers are always a wonderful thing. You feel validated as a business owner. But do you know what is even better? Repeat customers. Repeat customers are the backbone of any solid business. These people come back to your business because their first experience with the product or service was a success. They received more value than they paid for. If you don't convert *new* customers to *repeat* customers, you will soon see your sales numbers start to fall precipitously.

This is obvious in a tech startup that charges a monthly or annual fee—which is by far the most common pricing model. But this is also very true for every other type of business, even if it is not subscription-based. Realtors, retirement advisors, insurance brokers, landscaping services, delicatessen restaurants ("delis"), and more all need recurring revenue to survive.

Let's use a deli as an example of how important repeat customers are to profits.

- The owner of a deli decides to invest in a marketing blitz in the month of January, buying radio ads, a billboard placement, and handing out coupon flyers at the local farmers market.

- In February, she sees a surge of new customers use the coupon flyer at the deli—100 to be exact.
- She spent $5,000 on her marketing campaign, which means she paid $50 ($5,000 / 100) for each new customer.
- The average customer spends $25 on an order. A customer must therefore come to the deli *at least* twice ($25 X 2) in order for the deli owner to break even on her marketing investment.
- For every customer that doesn't come back, she will have paid $25 to lose that customer. Not a good deal, right?

This example illustrates how important winning loyal customers is to a business. The method to loyal customers? Onboarding. Through onboarding, you ensure that your customers have a fantastic experience on their early interactions with your product or service. You help them get "on board" with what you are doing. First impressions are everything—and in most cases, they are within your control.

The best place to start when designing an onboarding approach is at the end. For the deli, the ideal end is a customer sitting at a table enjoying a sandwich that perfectly matches what they craved. With that kind of experience, the customer is likely to come back again and maybe tell others about the value.

So, you start with the perfect outcome—the customer enjoying a perfect sandwich. What actions can the deli owner take to ensure that happens for every new customer, every time? Maybe the deli owner creates a separate register station just for new customers where someone knowledgeable about the menu can help consult with the new diner on his or her selection. Maybe she also provides samples of sauce and cheese options to puzzled new customers. Maybe she creates a separate menu for first-timers that answers the "what is popular here?" question proactively.

Through trial and error, the deli owner can find the recipe to delight new customers and convert them to loyal ones.

How do I ensure customers have a great experience?

Bottom Line

Attraction to your new business is important. Retention is even more important. If you design a solid onboarding of *new* customers to your business at the beginning, you will start to build momentum that might surprise you.

How do I know much to spend on marketing?
(LTV vs. CAC)

19

How do I know how much I should spend on marketing?

When starting your business, it is normal to get fixated on the "launch." It is exciting, and it is what is right in front of you. The marketing tasks on your to-do list are all very likely related to getting the word out at the beginning. But the marketing effort that will make your startup a "stayup" is likely not tied to your launch strategy. The key question is in fact: How will you predictably and profitably attract new customers to your business on an ongoing basis?

To solve this riddle, you will be tempted to start doing what you see everyone else doing. Or, if you've started a business before, you will be tempted to go back to your old bag of tricks. Social media? Check. Flyers? Check. Great website? Check. Suddenly, you're spending a lot of money. It may work *if* you get lucky. However, your success will more likely come down to your ability to understand and apply two tools that are commonly discussed and applied in tech startups.

Tech Startup Term: "LTV (Lifetime Value) vs. CAC (Customer Acquisition Cost)"

How do I know how much I should spend on marketing?

***Startup for Everyone* Translation:** A calculation to ensure that the money you spend to attract a customer is less than the money that customer will pay your business over time.

You have to generate more money than you spend to win each new customer. This may seem obvious, but it is surprising how many businesses do not think this way. LTV and CAC calculations give you insight into whether or not this is happening. Data doesn't lie, so the tools gained significant traction in tech startups because throwing money at marketing and hoping for the best, or "spray and pray," became very popular for a while. While fun for startup founders, investors felt like their money was being lit on fire.

So, what are LTV and CAC? Some quick definitions to get us going:

Lifetime Value = The average transaction value from each customer **multiplied by** the number of times you expect him or her to make a transaction **multiplied by** length of time you expect the average customer to *stay* a customer.

Coffee Shop Example: **$4.00** (average transaction) x **ten times per month** (number of transactions) x **twelve months** (time as customer) = **$480.00** (4 x 10 x 12)

This means that when a new customer decides to start frequenting your coffee shop in a *typical/average* way, you can expect to generate $480 from that customer.

Customer Acquisition Cost = Total dollars spent on marketing your business (including your time) **divided by** number of new customers.

Coffee Shop Example:

(Because I used months as the time metric in LTV, I'll use monthly amounts in this calculation.) In January, you spent:

$100 on posters + **$300** on coupons + **$500** on Facebook ads + **$1,000** worth of your time = **$1,900**

You won 10 new customers in January, and $1,900 / 10 = **$190** to acquire each new customer.

This is good news! Each customer will generate $480 of revenue, and it only cost you $190 to acquire each one. Your business will be left with $290 to spend on operating expenses and/or profits. If this equation resulted in a negative number, then you would either need to increase price, increase transactions, make your customers more loyal, OR reduce your marketing expenses.

This concept is key to understanding if a business (or the strategy it is taking) is viable and sustainable. There are a lot of stories of tech startups that ran this calculation and found it shockingly out of whack (e.g. spending more money than they were making). Don't do that. Run the numbers.

Every business is different; this concept is not a "copy and paste" exercise. You, as the founder, must sit down and think this through for *your* business. A realtor might find it completely financially acceptable to spend $1,000 entertaining a potential client in order to win business. In the case of the coffee shop, that would make no sense.

Bottom Line
While this approach might seem overly tactical, it is critical. If you ever try to raise money from a sophisticated investor, they will ask you for your CAC and LTV. Don't get stuck without the answer. It is a core building block of anything successful—with or without investors.

How do I know the right time to "go big"?
(Product-Market Fit)

20

How do I know the right time to "go big"?

There is no shortage these days of inspirational content trying to convince you to "go all in" with your idea. The message resonates because most of us are drawn to the stories of people who muster up enough courage to take a big risk and silence the naysayers with a triumph. It is why we love movies where the underdog takes down the favorite or the hero overcomes against all odds. So how do you know when is the right time for you to increase your commitment to your business or idea?

As much as we secretly envision a glorious moment of breakthrough, we also dreadfully fear the potential failure. Believing in something is great, but how can you be sure you won't step out with courage, double down on the vision, and fall flat on your face? Or even worse, become overconfident in what you have to the point where you ignore fundamental flaws and overinvest in an underdeveloped concept? Unfortunately, startups fail often; and that failure is most commonly a result of one thing that goes wrong.

Tech Startup Term: "Product-Market Fit"

How do I know the right time to "go big"?

***Startup for Everyone* Translation:** Matching your solution perfectly with the people experiencing the need for what you are selling—making it irresistible to buy.

We all want our thing to work. Yet too many founders find themselves with slow sales and a mediocre response to their current product from customers. The natural temptation is to try to solve this problem by pouring in more marketing, more salespeople, more effort, or more new offerings to create some momentum. This results in what Steve Blank, well-known entrepreneur and investor, calls "premature scaling." Founders are in a hurry to be successful and start overcooking something that customers didn't want to eat in the first place. Instead of pouring in more resources too soon, you should dig deeper to discover the elements that would make your product or service *irresistible*. What would make your customers want to bring up what you have to offer in conversation at a dinner party?

In a customer's mind, Product-Market Fit translates to:

**Exactly what you made (Product) =
Exactly what I want (Market)**

Your product or service solves customers' problem or meets their need in such a way that they will buy it despite your ability to execute perfectly. When this happens, you can be relatively confident that *it is going to work* because *it is already working*.

Here are a **few characteristics** of a product or service that has arrived at this point:

1. You can't keep product on the shelves.
2. Your sales are growing with no marketing effort.
3. You are getting referrals regularly from "happy customers."
4. You don't have to negotiate price or contract terms.
5. *You* love your product and use it regularly.

This is the right time to scale, double down, and "go all in" on the business. You have found the magic recipe. Success will still require a lot of work, fine-tuning, and adjustments, but you've got something special. Now, your product needs greater commitment and investment from you and others to turn it into everything that it could be. Then the concern becomes more about managing growth than about creating it. Spending money on marketing is like pouring jet fuel on an already blazing fire.

Bottom Line

Create a great product that fits an explicit need for someone you care about and empathize with—and build from there. Get it to fly off the shelves, be the talk of the town, and be something you would use. Hit Product-Market Fit before trying to scale or invest too much. It sounds basic, but it is so easy to overlook when starting something new.

Bonus Chapter

Definitions on Additional Terms

There is a seemingly never-ending list of tech startup terms that need translation. I had to stop the book at some point, so I cut myself off at twenty. But I want to provide a quick *Startup for Everyone Translation* for an additional set of eleven terms.

CAP Table
A shorthand way to say, "capitalization table", which is a detailed breakdown (typically a spreadsheet or table) of the ownership structure (% or shares per owner) of the business.

MRR
An acronym for "monthly recurring revenue" or "annual recurring revenue" (ARR) that usually is a sign of how stable a business because it indicates the loyalty of customers.

EBIT
An acronym for "earnings before interest and taxes" that helps owners and investors understand profitability of the core activities of the business without interest and taxes deducted.

Lean Startup
A methodology coined by Eric Reis used to describe an approaching to building a product or service through the least amount of resources possible, incorporating feedback early.

Prototyping
The process of building an imperfect version of your early product, testing it with people, discovering what doesn't work, and then re-building new revised versions.

P&L
Accounting shorthand for your "profit and loss statement". This document shows how much money you made, how much you spent, and whether you made a profit or loss.

Balance Sheet
An accounting document that shows how much your business owns (cash, equipment, buildings, supplies, etc.) compared to how much you owe (loans, bills, etc.) at a given time.

Growth Hacking
A term used by tech startups to describe trying to market their product or services using little to no money. It is the practice of creatively finding cheap ways to build awareness quickly.

Bootstrapping
A concept taken from the saying, "Pull yourself up by your bootstraps." Therefore, "bootstrapping" refers to startups who are still building their company without outside investment.

Term Sheet
This is like an offer letter from an outside investor. It is a formal letter describing the amount of money to be invested with additional deal terms such as ownership percentage.

Pro Forma
This is business speak for financial projections for your business. Your "pro forma" is typically a spreadsheet that depicts what you anticipate *future* financial performance to be.

Closing
My hope for you

Before I decided to write this book, I searched for one like it. I had so many friends who were starting new things but lacked the confidence that entrepreneurs require to overcome the initial barriers to get started. I searched everywhere and could not find the book I needed. So, I resolved to fill the gap.

A barrage of questions filled my mind:
- Who would read it?
- Would people find it helpful?
- Would it be enough to overcome barriers?

As I write this closing, I still don't know the answer to those questions—but it doesn't matter. I can only focus on what I can control: *the work*. There is too much wisdom kept under the veil of tech jargon, and I felt a burden to reveal it. Like many entrepreneurs, I felt overwhelmed and intimidated and stuck.

One of my favorite quotes is from Steven Pressfield, author of *The War of Art*, who says, "We must do our work for its own sake, not for fortune or attention or applause." You should, too. Don't let your fear of getting it wrong be the only thing stopping you from doing something right. If you have identified a problem worth fixing, then you must move forward. Solve it, and move us all forward.

I hope you use the concepts in this book to build something you love and are proud of. Do the work.

About the Author

Casey Bankord has more than a decade of leadership and consulting experience with companies of all sizes. After ten years as a pastor, he founded and subsequently sold a digital publishing company. After he was admitted into an exclusive startup accelerator in Silicon Valley, Casey was identified as a top founder of his graduating class and recruited to coach other founders. In that role, he coached twelve startups and developed deep proficiencies in prototyping, customer validation, product design and development, financial modeling, branding and positioning, business model design, marketing strategy, and raising rounds of capital.

In 2014, Casey joined Clareo (www.clareo.com) to consult larger companies on startup methodologies, innovation mindset, and capabilities to deliver innovation performance. He has worked alongside senior executives at large companies in various industries, such as consumer packaged goods, building materials, mining, defense, food, media, healthcare, energy, and insurance. His work has spanned helping small, dedicated project teams in launching a new venture to facilitating 1000+ attendee events designed to generate innovative concepts. Casey also leads Clareo's rapidly growing software business, Forest (www.forestsoftware.com).

Casey holds an MBA from the Kellogg School of Management at Northwestern University, where he was the co-chair of the Honor Code Committee, keynote speaker for the entrepreneurship club, finalist for the New World Ventures (now Pritzker Group) LaunchU startup challenge, and was given the Dean's Distinguished Service award upon graduation for his outstanding service to the school. Casey lives in Wheaton, IL, outside Chicago, with his wife and three sons.

www.ingramcontent.com/pod-product-compliance
Lightning Source LLC
Chambersburg PA
CBHW070232220526

45465CB00004B/1400